DATING POTENTIAL

DATING POTENTIAL

Selah

XULON PRESS

Xulon Press
2301 Lucien Way #415
Maitland, FL 32751
407.339.4217
www.xulonpress.com

Paperback ISBN-13: 978-1-66286-663-0
Ebook ISBN-13: 978-1-66286-664-7

TABLE OF CONTENTS

Introduction

I've heard this phrase a lot growing up, "He or she has potential." Potential to be a good man or woman. Potential to be a good spouse. Potential to be a great athlete. Potential to be successful in business. Potential to be better or someone different than who they are when initially observed. I realized in some instances, the word "potential" has taken on a different form. No longer is it an adjective serving as the way we describe people. Instead, it has morphed into a noun, which is a person, place, or thing. In this case, "potential" is now a figurative person who a man or woman will date. What was once identified as a trait a person has that could trend in a positive direction eventually becomes the fixation of the man or woman observing them and personified. Once their potential is personified, it becomes the reason one enters in or remains in a relationship that is not God's best for their life.

The problem I've concluded is this: We think a person is going to change, or they say they're going to change, and many times they don't. In some instances, they actually do change, and that's great! But in others, there's no permanence of change, and that can be a factor to really evaluate. Was the reason for the change genuine, or was it used to manipulate the direction of the relationship? I'm not saying you should look for perfection—that can only be found in Christ. But I am saying don't settle for Mr. or Ms. Potential.

Although people may grow and change in various areas of their lives, I must emphasize how critical it is to take notes and truthfully weigh whether or not you should remain connected with or eventually marry that individual. Our hope in them becoming the best version of themselves is not enough. There must be evidence of actions being taken for self-improvement.

Some time ago, I was considering dating a guy who made his intentions known that he was interested in me and was looking to marry one day. After learning this, I spent time getting to know and observing him. At that time, he <u>seemed</u> to be pursuing Christ and growing spiritually. I recall a conversation I had with one of my mentors. I told her what I believed the Lord had shown me about him, and it was good! It was an area of his life that could develop and change. I'll never forget her response: "What if he doesn't change?" I knew he would have to cooperate with the plan and will of God for his life in order to obtain what God had revealed to not just me, but also to him and others in his life as well. Yet, the potential for change was there.

Well, we eventually entered into a relationship, but I quickly realized there was no effort to develop—none to develop spiritually, and none to move toward who God had called him to be. Also, there were other contributing factors that drove a wedge in the relationship. As a result, I had to make a decision: Would I be with him because of his potential, or would I leave based off of what I knew to be true?

This book is not comprehensive in what areas to think through when entering into relationships, but by the leading of the Holy Spirit, I am presenting some significant themes to consider. Equally important is that you assess yourself and make sure you apply these and other principles to your daily living before requiring them of others in a relationship. Let's dive in!

Chapter 1

CREATOR

Genesis 1:26-27 (NIV)

> *26 Then God said, "Let us make mankind in our image, in our likeness, so that they may rule over the fish in the sea and the birds in the sky, over the livestock and all the wild animals, and over all the creatures that move along the ground." 27 So God created mankind in his own image, in the image of God he created them; male and female he created them.*

People have many ideas about who or what "makes" or "made" them who they are. Money, careers, some kind of success in life, other people, etc., these are things or ways some people gain a *false* sense of identity. The downfall is that if or when the identifier is removed, there can be a grave impact on the individual. God says in His Word that He made us in **His** image and likeness, so no matter what one has or doesn't have, it is important to know where your identity comes from.

Although fame, success, or other accomplishments can make us more recognizable and bring pleasure to some sphere of our lives, the truth is that God created all of us, and it is important for the person you desire to marry to know this. We must independently place high value on the knowledge of our Creator so that when the storms of life come and sweep away people or things around us, we don't lose ourselves in the process. Further, knowing our Creator can prevent us from turning to destructive habits that may lead to further injury or even death. When people's identities are tied to what they have, loss comes with the loss of an identity not given by God.

One biblical example of someone who was able to stand in the face of grave adversity was Job. Though he lost everything, including his children, he didn't lose himself. On the other hand, Job's wife looked at his loss in a different light. Her response was to curse God and die **(Job 2:9)**. This may serve as one indicator of her view of their life and possessions. Without minimizing their experience, it's easy to criticize her for her response and lack of commitment to God.

Yet, it is so real how people can become despondent in hard times. Instead of looking to their Creator for help, answers, or understanding, she took the extreme view that Job's life was no longer valuable because what was valuable to him was gone. *Side bar* ... Why didn't she take her own advice if she felt that way about Job? **(More to follow in Chapter 4: His Connections.)**

Being created in our Father's image and likeness means we should resemble Him. Consider parent-child relationships; we tend to see resemblances in a parent and child's appearance, speech, and even behavior. Sometimes, the resemblance and/or behaviors are so strikingly similar that others can tell who a child belongs to because of what they observe, even when his or her parents are not around.

In the same way, when we are born again, we should begin to look like our Father. When people claim the name

2

of Christ, there should be corresponding actions in their lives that let others know whose child they are. Do you know what the Father looks like? If so, then when you meet people, you should be able to identify whether or not they look like Him. This is imperative as believers who say we want to marry another believer.

First and foremost, can you be identified as a believer? It's not enough to just say you are. Next, when you meet a man or woman, can you honestly evaluate by biblical standards whether or not they are a true follower of Christ, a child of God? For example, Jesus said that people will know we are His disciples by the love we have for one another **(John 13:35)**. Can you see the love? *Saying* one is a follower, believer, or child of God is one thing. *Being* one is another.

We often mistake people who call themselves believers as being ones. But I like an analogy one of my former pastors shared. People can say they are on a certain sports team, but if they're not wearing an assigned jersey, showing up to practice, and knowing the plays that are called, it's evident that they are not really on that team. This is a practical way to demolish the epidemic going around that everyone who *says* they are a Christian *is* a Christian. People can say what they want, but at the end of the day, every team member has a jersey, and EVERY tree is identified by the fruit it bears **(Luke 6:43-45)**.

In conclusion, let's take time to examine ourselves and be honest. Are we merely saying we are children of the most-high God, or are we truly living lives reflective of being His sons and daughters? Next, is the person we're considering for marriage also a true child of God? If a paternity test was performed, what would the results be? Do any of you remember *The Maury Povich Show*? If not, maybe a modern version of this would be

Paternity Court. When the paternity test comes back on either one of those shows, what would the answer be?

> "God, You ARE the Father!" or "God, You ARE NOT the Father!"

Chapter 2

CHURCH

Hebrews 10:24-25 (NKJV)

> *24 And let us consider one another in order to stir up love and good works, 25 not forsaking the assembling of ourselves together, as is the manner of some, but exhorting one another, and so much the more as you see the Day approaching.*

K nowing whether or not the person you are dating and/or considering for marriage is connected to a local church is of utmost importance as a believer. I'm not talking about someone who used to, sometimes goes, or "wants" to go to church. Why? you may ask. Well, building upon the foundation of Chapter 1, being a part of a church is a major part of how our Creator wants us to navigate this journey called life while here on earth. One reason can be seen in the verse above. *"We are to stir up love and good works"* and *"exhort one another."* These, among other things, are what we should be experiencing when we come together.

Being a member of a church reflects how God sees us. **In 1 Corinthians 12:12-14 (NIV), it states, "¹² Just as a body, though one, has many parts, but all its many parts form one** body, so it is with Christ. **¹³ For we were all baptized by one Spirit so as to form one body—whether Jews or Gentiles, slave or free—and we were all given the one Spirit to drink. ¹⁴ Even so the body is not made up of one part but of many."** Verse 27 goes on to say, **"²⁷ Now you are the body of Christ, and each one of you is a part of it."**

"Going to church" is what many refer to as the act of going to a building for a worship service. For clarity, WE are the body of Christ. That is what makes US the church, not the building in which we meet. *(This can be understood as you read more about the church in the New Testament. Some books in the Bible to reference are Matthew, Acts, and Romans.)* Even more, there are so many meaningful reasons God wants us to come together; to be equipped for the work of the ministry **(Eph. 4:11-13)**, to be encouraged, to hear from Him, and so much more!

So, what about those who don't attend services? Well, my introductory scripture lets us know that one who forsakes the assembly is disobeying God's Word (even virtually). He explicitly states not to do that. To add to that, each part of the body has a purpose that is beneficial for the other parts. This excites me because contrary to how some view church, the pastor and select other members are not the only valuable members of the body of Christ. In 1 Corinthians 12 you will see great details regarding the various works of service administered by the Spirit of God to EACH person. This includes me and you!

The works of service mentioned above can also be referred to as "spiritual gifts." When you think about it in the natural sense, imagine if you showed up to a friend's birthday party every year with a gift in your hand but your friend never showed up. I imagine that's what it looks like in the spiritual realm when we all do not come together as a body of believers. The gifts in others are made for you to partake of. Likewise, the gift(s) in you is supposed to be shared with others. But if no one comes together, how can they be given or received? Often what ends up happening is the same few people keep exchanging gifts amongst each other. In those cases, the gifts are intended to be shared among so many more people. There should be a constant exchange, a flow (of spiritual gifts) between us as believers. And this is not limited to the sanctuary in which you meet. I implore you to ensure that you and whomever you choose to connect with are active members of the church because "There is something in you that God needs to get to other people" (Pastor Valkeith Williams). What an honor to be used by the Almighty God for His good works!

Several years ago, I was talking to a co-worker about dating, and she asked me how frequently I expected a man to go to church. My response was basically, "Every Sunday." For the record, that is and was a reflection of my participation, in addition to Bible study and volunteer activities. Then she asked, "What if he wants to stay home and watch the game on Sunday?" I don't recall my exact response, but there are various ones I have for a question like that. Nevertheless, I did not agree with her view that that was okay. Her follow-up response was, "Everyone can't be like you."

Consider this: What if the pastor or other leaders wanted to stay home too? What if we all were inconsistent and did our own thing without rhyme or reason? What if no one had any true commitment to God or the body of Christ? How would that profit us? I was strongly exhorted early in my walk with Christ to honor the God Who gives us life, Who wakes us up, gives us health and strength, gives us the ability to generate wealth **(Deut. 8:18)**, and provides abundantly for us daily.

Typically, local churches have a minimum of one or two corporate services a week, while many of us go to work or school approximately five days a week for up to eight hours a day. So out of the seven days a week that we have, why can't we corporately give God one to two days to fellowship with other believers for a few hours? I understand things come up, and sometimes there are schedule conflicts. But Jesus sacrificed His life for us to give us eternal life. Let's give Him honor where honor is due. One way we can do that is not to forsake coming together in His name.

Going back to the point of this chapter, if we are saved and name the name of Christ, we become members of His body who make up His church. (The church is not the building we go to for our meetings or services. Rather, it is comprised of the men and women who are believers in Jesus Christ and are children of God.) Does the person you're considering have a body of believers he or she is attached to? If you don't know yet, ask. Take his or her spiritual temperature. One question I like to ask is, "How are you doing spiritually?" Another question is, "What did you learn today during service?" In all your "getting," get understanding **(Pro. 4:7 KJV)**.

Below are some suggested points I'd like to suggest you observe, ask, and/or discuss when considering someone for a relationship. WARNING: Be prepared to also be observed, asked the same questions, and/or have the same discussions directed toward you. These are areas you want to make sure align between you.

- Are they a member of a local church?

- If so, do they regularly attend?

- Are they actively involved?

- How do they interact with other members?

- Talk about the Bible and its lessons.

    o What are they learning?

- Application of the Word of God.

    o What ways does the Word change their life/impact their home?

- Are they growing spiritually?

- Do they understand how to hear from God?

- Do they hear from God?

- Do they pray?

Having a relationship with Christ and being a member of a local church takes priority over being in a relationship with a man or woman. God should be first place, and no one and nothing else should come before Him. I know this doesn't work out in all scenarios, as I understand that in some instances, people date or marry and later, one or both come to know the Lord. In lieu of that, Christ is still the priority. Now, if you are not married, make Him your first priority, then verify if He is a true priority for the person you're considering, not just a thought in his or her head. After all, God created marriage, and He knows exactly what we need in order to be successful when coming together as one. God also knows what we'll need to maintain what **He** joins together.

I grew up "going to church," and I always left feeling good because I did what I thought was right in the sight of God. Yet, I really wasn't learning and retaining much. I lived my life based off of my own moral compass of what behaviors were good and bad. When I was in my early twenties, that's when my relationship with Christ really went to a new level. Some people would call that having a "true conversion experience." I was a disciple for the first time in my life. I received assistance purchasing a study Bible, and I studied that Bible! I learned how to pray, began applying the biblical principles of the Word of God to my life, and put my hands to the plow by getting involved on various ministry teams. All the while, God was doing a new work in me.

I did not want to be single any longer. I wanted to get married but just hadn't met the right person. I believe God had me hidden for that period of time in my life for a few reasons. 1) I had self-esteem issues, so He had to show me who I am and Whose I am. 2) I had deep-rooted family issues I needed to overcome. 3) I not only needed healing but also deliverance in different areas of my life. I could go on and on, but it's not necessary in this book. I always tell people, especially other singles, that I appreciated my time of singleness. I was able to serve God with undivided loyalty (1 Cor. 7:35). Also, I realized that whoever I met and married would not have to deal with *some* of my baggage. I'm still growing and changing, so there's no perfection here.

For years, I listened to messages about marriage and saw many successful and unsuccessful marriages in church. Through this, I was able to understand marriage better and deeper than the way the world painted it to me before my conversion experience. I gained better direction when it came to what a wife was and should be in accordance to the Bible. I intend to walk that out with the help and direction from the Word of God and other happily married Christians (the church).

I said all of the above to say this: If it hadn't been for me connecting to local bodies of Christ (in the various cities I've lived in) that discipled me, I would not be who I am today. There's nothing wrong with watching other ministers and pastors on television. Reading Christian books is also great! But this is only supplemental to the church God calls you to join (*including a virtual church*). Nevertheless, you should be growing and changing for the better while being equipped for the work of the ministry.

It is essential that we are in fellowship with one another. And as I mentioned before, there's value in coming together. Please do not forsake the assembly of believers. We all need each other, as God intricately designed His body to operate as one unit, with each part having a special function. We're stronger and better together! So, I leave you with this question: Is the person you're considering a member of the body of Christ, or is it something he or she just talks about becoming a part of?

Chapter 3

CHARACTER

Colossians 3:12 (NKJV)

Character of the New Man

> *Therefore, as the elect of God, holy and beloved,*
> *put on tender mercies, kindness, humility,*
> *meekness, longsuffering...*

Character – (noun) The combination of traits and qualities distinguishing the individual nature of a person or thing. one such distinguishing quality; characteristic. moral force; integrity a man of character. Reputation, especially a good reputation **(Dictionary.com).**

L et's discuss the importance of the qualities of the inner person, who people are at their core—their personality traits and character. Then, as a subtopic, I want to tie in whether or not this makes them compatible and, subsequently, suitable for you.

Why is character so important? First and foremost, it matters to God. The old man (before Christ) behaves one way, but the new man (in Christ) is a new creation and does not exhibit behaviors of the former. In Colossians 3:12 (NKJV), we see that there are qualities that we who belong to God should exhibit. It doesn't just happen arbitrarily; the Bible says to "put on" these things. It's a deliberate action we must do on a daily basis. But I want to suggest that before we put on new character, we must take off the old character.

For instance, apart from Christ, you may be impatient and rude, but in Christ, God wants you to disrobe from the former and put on longsuffering (which is patience) and kindness. I say "disrobe" because we don't put new things on top of old things. Who puts newer, cleaner clothes on top of old clothes? You won't look right, the clothes won't fit properly, and at some point, the way you're supposed to maneuver will get impaired because you have on way too much. To add to that, you may not have on the right items for the weather or occasion.

Here's another way to look at this. Let's say you are a construction worker, but you show up to the job site in business casual attire. This is not befitting for your role. You've now put yourself in a situation to be harmed in that environment. You need a construction hat, steel toe boots, appropriate eyewear, and, perhaps, other protective gear. In a similar way, God wants us, as His elect, holy and beloved, to put on the right attire— character. And He makes available to us the attire we need for every occasion and for every season.

Although the scripture talks about "putting on" character, it is a metaphor for how we should acquire what God desires for us to exude from the inside out. When you think about it, many of us are members of teams, organizations, programs, or companies that prioritize character as a positive quality they want reflected from us. **It matters in the world, so why not make it our priority to put on godly character?** Let's take a look at a scripture reflecting the importance of the inward man to God.

7 But the Lord said to Samuel, "Do not con-
sider his appearance or his height, for I have
rejected him. The Lord does not look at the
things people look at. People look at the out-
ward appearance, but the Lord looks at the
heart." (1 Samuel 16:7 NIV)

In this passage, the Lord sent the prophet Samuel to the house of Jesse to look for the next king. Jesse presented all but one of his sons to Samuel. As Samuel looked upon Jesse's son Eliab, he thought he had identified the next one who was anointed to be king. But the Lord felt otherwise. This passage goes on to explain how David, the son Jesse left out from the initial presentation, was eventually brought before the prophet. His physical appearance was not impressive by the standards perhaps associated with a king. However, God did not evaluate David by his outward appearance. He assessed what was in his heart. As a result, he was the one whom God called and anointed for the task!

Often in our society, we put too much emphasis on the outward appearance. Though physical attraction is where it begins for most, the character of a person is often overlooked or not assessed with the same weight as the physical or other outward qualities and possessions of a person. I recall dating a young man who outwardly had all the makings to be a husband. He was attractive, well dressed, and had a nice house, car, and well-paying job. However, as I got to know him more, I realized he was very immature. I remember feeling like I was dating someone in junior high. Now, I won't divulge our ages at the time, but let's just say we were far removed from our teenage years. The way he thought, perceived things, responded to issues, pursued Christ (or lack thereof), and behaved on the job and in his personal life were all things I weighed in my decision to cease the relationship. There were qualities of his character that I felt were not acceptable for someone I was dating and considering for marriage. Despite those close to him discouraging some of the behaviors, he didn't change. He had the potential to be a husband, but based upon his character, I determined he was neither compatible with me nor a suitable man for my lifestyle.

Compatibility – (noun) The natural ability to live or work together in harmony because of well-matched characteristics; the quality or fact of being in agreement; consistency (dictionary.com).

The Bible says in **Amos 3:3 (NLT), "Can two people walk together without agreeing on the direction?"** When assessing your mate, you should evaluate what level of agreement you walk in. Where do you stand when it comes to your belief system, finances, personal fitness, family, etc.? If there is little to no agreement regarding spiritual and fundamental principles you possess as individuals, how can your relationship move in a direction that is both positive and productive? When there is no agreement, you'll find that you'll often move in different directions or not move at all once it comes down to matters that can be either simple or weighty.

You can look at compatibility two ways: 1) How much do you agree about a matter? 2) If your thoughts or actions are not the same, do they complement each other in a way that brings harmony to a situation? For instance, financial health may be important to both people in the relationship, but one person may be better at writing and managing a budget while the other is good at shopping for quality products that are budget-friendly by using coupons, finding deals, and not overspending.

Suitable – (adjective) such as to suit; appropriate; fitting; becoming (dictionary.com).

Seeing this word immediately makes me think of God when He spoke to Adam in the Garden of Eden.

[18] The LORD God said, "It is not good for the man to be alone. I will make a helper **suitable** for him." [19] Now the LORD God had formed out of the ground all the wild animals and all the birds in the sky. He brought them to the man to see what he would name them; and whatever the man called each living creature, that was its name. [20] So the man gave names to all the livestock, the birds in the sky and all the wild animals. But for Adam no **suitable helper** was found. [21] So the LORD God caused the man to fall into a deep sleep; and while he was sleeping, he took one of the man's ribs and then closed up the place with flesh. [22] Then the LORD God made a woman from the rib he had taken out of the man, and he brought her to the man. (**Genesis 2:18-22 NIV**)

When God looked at Adam, He saw that not only was he alone but that none of the creation around him were suitable for him. The animals he named were not appropriate or fitting for a human relationship. Also, Adam needed someone to help him with the work God had given him to do. Enter Eve. Now they were able to work together and populate the earth. There is so much that can be extracted from the passage above regarding how we approach our assessment of the man or woman we consider being joined to, but there are two things I'll point out. First, can we identify if the man has a God-given assign-ment/job? What is the woman coming alongside of him to help with? (This may or may not be determined up front.) Second, if having children is a desire you both have, can you see yourself starting a family with one another?

As I mentioned in my introduction, character, compatibility, and suitability are all intertwined. Throughout the Bible, we can learn from various scriptures the type of character God desires for us to exude. As we strive to be the godly men and women we are called to be, it's appropriate for us to also evaluate the character of the people we date and marry. Again, we're not looking at who they can become, but rather, who they are today. Do they walk in integrity? Do they have a good reputation? Have they put on the character of the new man? Also, is there compatibility between you? Do your morals, goals, and spiri-tual views align in a way that brings harmony to the relation-ship? Finally, are you suitable, or fitting, for one another as it pertains to the call on your lives and purpose God has for you?

God has new apparel for us when we come to know Him through Christ. As believers, let's look how our Father wants us to look. He's given us the new apparel; it's up to us to put it on!

Chapter 4

CONNECTIONS

Psalm 1:1-3 (NKJV)

The Way of the Righteous and the End of the Ungodly

> *1 Blessed is the man who <u>walks not</u> in the counsel of the ungodly, <u>nor stands</u> in the path of sinners, <u>nor sits</u> in the seat of the scornful; 2 But his delight is in the law of the Lord, and in His law he meditates day and night. 3 He shall be like a tree Planted by the rivers of water, that brings forth its fruit in its season, whose leaf also shall not wither; and whatever he does shall prosper.*

When coming to Christ, sometimes it can be hard to separate from old friends and loved ones who are not people God wants you to remain close to. Nevertheless, He will ask you to make that decision for Him. Also to be considered is who we forge new friendships with. This may not be true for all relationships, but the Bible is very clear about who we as believers should and should not be connected to. In the scripture above, it says we are not to walk in the counsel of the ungodly or stand in the path of sinners or sit in the seat of the scornful.

19

My question is this: Who are you walking, standing, and sitting with? This allows a certain proximity to others that can impact what you hear, what you say, how you behave, and more, especially if these interactions are on a frequent basis. And in case you're wondering, "What about locations like work and school or other places you have to be around unbelievers?" Well, your posture is not only physical but also mental. For instance, there have been some conversations at work that I chose not to join in on. When I've had the opportunity to walk away, I've walked away, moved seats, or let it be known I was no longer interested in discussing a matter. Other times, I've redirected conversations, put on headphones, invited someone else to start a new conversation with me while others continued to talk, prayed under my breath, you get the gist. There are ways to avoid making connections with people in situations that are not fruitful for a believer when you're in environments you cannot avoid.

So, what about people you're considering for a relationship? Who are they always around? This chapter is so important to me because I recall being in friendships and relationships where the men I associated with had connections I did not need to be in proximity to. When I was younger, I recall having close friends, and I did not think much about who their friends were because to some extent, we all ran in the same circles. However, when I came to Christ, I became more aware of the impact my friends' connections had on me. Often, it wasn't my friends who were the issue; it was their friends who had a way with words and behaviors that were not appropriate. So, I severed some friendships due to their connections. Now, when I was not a godly woman, I did not realize the impact of my friends' friends because I had no spiritual discernment or conviction of some of the things going on around me.

In regard to some of my dating relationships, I've had to separate from men because who they were connected to was a point of contention. These men were so hard pressed about remaining connected to the wrong people that it frustrated me. When I say, "wrong people," I mean friends or family. In one case, one of the young men was being used by family for their personal gain. In another instance, the guy I was in a relationship with was constantly around people who argued, used profanity toward their spouse or others, raised their children absent of the biblical principles of God, drank *excessively*, you get my drift. It was not that I had a problem with their friends and loved ones. I loved them all dearly. My concern was the amount of time these men desired to be involved in these relationships while simultaneously wanting to expose me to them. Now, this was very hard to contend with because these relationships were deeply meaningful in their eyes. But they were not fruitful for us individually or our relationship. The people were not compelled by them to come out of darkness, yet the guys were so insistent on maintaining connection due to history or familial ties.

By contrast, I've been in a relationship where the young man was more aware of the people in certain environments and stated he would not take me around them. He covered me and my virtue because he knew those were situations I would not be comfortable in and were not good for either one of us. Again, love the people, but the atmosphere was not one we knew would be wise to put ourselves in. Also, we were in agreement about spending time with other Christians and believed that group dating would be beneficial for us as we continued to get to know each other. We valued being around people who would hold us accountable to remaining pure and also knew that good dialogue would come about from being in fellowship with other married couples.

The Bibles says in 1 Corinthians 15:33 (NIV), "Do not be deceived: 'Evil <u>company</u> corrupts good habits.'" There are many other sayings about the impact on a person's life as a result of who he or she spends time with. For instance:

1) "Birds of a feather flock together."

2) "Tell me who your friends are, and I'll show you where you are going."

3) "You can't separate yourself from who you spend time with."

So, what is the proverbial feather that keeps you bonded? Does it need to be plucked? I pause for effect …

That has more to do with you and not so much with the people you're around. If there is something we have in common with the world that needs to die (be plucked), it must go! As our minds are renewed and our lives are transformed in Christ, our interests and actions should change. This can be a hard conversation to have with others we need to separate from because many of us have may have deep history with them. In some cases, those relationships need to be severed, while in others, they may not.

Some may argue, "Jesus was a friend of sinners and tax collectors." This is true. But one, Jesus had a purpose in their lives. He did not go around them to be like them and/or to tolerate their sin. He called people to Himself, and CHANGE occurred. If it did not, I don't know any record of Him sticking around. Not only was/is He a friend, but He is also the Savior. People's lives hinge on how they respond to Him as the Savior of the world. Likewise, God may call us to be a friend to some who are not like us for the purpose of being salt and light in their lives. The goal is ultimately salvation through Jesus Christ. It really comes down to knowing the will of God for your life and recognizing when God does not have purpose for those relationships you desire to maintain. Yes, God uses us as Christians to reach/minister to those around us, but that takes knowing who you are called to.

The Bible speaks clearly about these things. No one has it all right. Make sure you have a word from God when it comes down to who you connect to and call a friend. I'll also add that there's got to be value placed on having and maintaining godly relationships with other Christians, especially those who are even more mature than you. Who we ultimately should be connected to is Christ. He is the True Vine. What I encourage you to evaluate is this:

1) When spending time with others, who is the majority of their time spent with?

2) People/objects: What has their attention outside of God, and how much influence/control does it have in their life/time?

3) Can you see yourself spending time with their friends?

4) If they are connected to the wrong crowd, are they willing to disconnect for Jesus?

5) Are they connected to idols?

In Chapter 1, I mentioned the relationship between Job and his wife. Let's discuss their connection. In Job chapters 1 and 2,

Satan received permission from God to test Job. This included stealing and destroying his animals, killing his servants and children, and inflicting his body with disease in order to "prove" to God that Job would curse God. (Please read these chapters for more insight.) With all of these things happening, Job did not curse God. After Job was struck with boils, this is how his wife responded: "⁹ His wife said to him, 'Are you still trying to maintain your integrity? Curse God and die.'" I like Job's response: "¹⁰ But Job replied, '**You talk like a foolish woman**. Should we accept only good things from the hand of God and never anything bad?' So in all this, Job said nothing wrong."

Now, to my understanding, there's no indication for us biblically to know how Job's wife viewed God before all of these tragedies that took place. Maybe she thought more of God when there was no trouble. Perhaps these events made her feel the way she did. Or, she may not have feared God as much as Job. Up until these tests, Job was a very rich, God-fearing man. Despite everything that had happened to him, he did not curse God. Yet, his wife was of the opinion that because all of these things had happened to him, there was no use in "maintaining his integrity."

Verse 9 in the Amplified version reads, "⁹ Then his wife said to him, 'Do you still cling to your integrity [and your faith and trust in God, without blaming Him]? Curse God and die!'" My first thought as I was writing this book was, "Why didn't SHE curse God and die?" These things did not solely happen to her husband; they happened to her too, right? At least, that's what I'm gathering. Why was it that Job lost HIS children and HIS livestock? It could have been stated that way because Job was the one being tested. Nevertheless, this loss should have had an impact on her as well; yet, she was not offering to take her own counsel.

My question for you is this: When both good and bad happen in our lives, what are the people we are connected to saying, especially about God? Are they blaming God? Have they lost faith in Him? Do they want us to turn our backs on Him? Have you had an opportunity to learn this about who you're considering to marry? You may not have been around to see the highs and lows, but it's good to talk about these things that have happened in your lives. Get an understanding of how they've responded when they were in their valleys. This is important. It's hard to really get the full understanding of how people will respond in future events, but sometimes, the past can be an indication of where they presently are in their walk and can offer some perspective for the future. God looked at Job and told Satan that he would not curse Him. Job had a reputation with God, and God had confidence that he would not turn away from Him. This is critical. We can gather from past performance what future performance may look like. Not that anyone walks through hardships perfectly and consistently, but will they remain connected to the True Vine?

Additional scripture for meditation:

John 15:1-8 (NLT): Jesus, the True Vine

> 15 "I am the true grapevine, and my Father is the gardener. ² He cuts off every branch of mine that doesn't produce fruit, and he prunes the branches that do bear fruit so they will produce even more. ³ You have already been pruned

and purified by the message I have given you.
[4] Remain in me, and I will remain in you. For a
branch cannot produce fruit if it is severed from
the vine, and you cannot be fruitful unless you
remain in me. [5] Yes, I am the vine; you are the
branches. Those who remain in me, and I in
them, will produce much fruit. For apart from
me you can do nothing. [6] Anyone who does
not remain in me is thrown away like a useless
branch and withers. Such branches are gathered
into a pile to be burned. [7] But if you remain in
me and my words remain in you, you may ask
for anything you want, and it will be granted! [8]
When you produce much fruit, you are my true
disciples. This brings great glory to my Father."

Not only are our earthly connections important, but most of
all, our connection to Jesus Christ is imperative to remain intact.

Chapter 5

CLOSET

Matthew 6:6 (KJV)

6 But thou, when thou prayest, enter into thy closet, and when thou hast shut thy door, pray to thy Father which is in secret; and thy Father which seeth in secret shall reward thee openly.

CONTRAST WITH:

Matthew 6:5 (NKJV)

5 "And when you pray, you shall not be like the hypocrites. For they love to pray <u>standing in the synagogues and on the corners of the streets, that they may be seen by men.</u> Assuredly, I say to you, <u>they have their reward.</u>

A s you probably have gathered by now, the title of this chapter is not referring to the contents within one's bedroom closet: clothes, shoes, accessories, etc. Though, that is something to consider about your mate as well. Instead, we're going to discuss the importance of prayer in the life of the person you're considering. Learning whether or not a person prays may take time, depending on the circumstances in which you meet. Nevertheless, one's prayer life is a significant aspect to know about because it will be both essential and instrumental in marriage just as it is in your single lives.

While God's hierarchy is established as Christ being the head of every man and man the head of the woman (**1 Cor. 11:3 NLT**), ladies you need to know that he's not only covered by God but also that he hears from God. After all, everything begins with the head. Decisions are made, instructions are provided/received, and then everything else follows. This is what makes prayer essential and instrumental for our daily lives. It is of utmost importance that you know where his directions come from. Does it come from his own thinking, emotions, and reactions to situations, or is God pointing him in the direction he should go with Holy Spirit as his guide? This is significant because you need to be able to assess whether or not he is someone you can both submit to and follow under God.

Our best example of how to have a healthy prayer life comes from Jesus Christ. You'll see in Luke 5:16 (NIV) where Jesus withdrew to lonely places to pray. A little background … As people learned more about Jesus, they came to hear Him speak and be healed of their sicknesses and diseases. However, He would often withdraw from the crowds to spend time in prayer. What can we infer was happening when Jesus spent time alone with God? Conversation, rest, replenishment, receipt of instructions, and more. What can we take away from this passage? We don't need to continuously expend ourselves without taking time to go before God in prayer. What's also rich is that this ties into the opening scripture. Jesus spent time doing business with God in secret. To this day, His reward is so substantial that we are perpetually beneficiaries of the blessings bestowed upon Him.

John 5:19-20 (NIV) shows us how Jesus responded to God's direction:

> [19] Jesus gave them this answer: "Very truly I tell you, the Son can do nothing by himself; he can do only what he sees his Father doing, because whatever the Father does the Son also does. [20] For the Father loves the Son and shows him all he does. Yes, and he will show him even greater works than these, so that you will be amazed.

I whole-heartedly believe that just as God reveals to Jesus what He should do, God will and does the same for us. When it comes to considering future spouses, if you don't know, ask them if they pray. Talk about some of the things God is showing and telling you both to do. Don't just assume that they're praying. If you're considering someone and you have not reached the point of discussing this matter, one indicator of his or her obedience to God can be assessed by the decisions he or she makes and the corresponding results. When observing them making decisions, do they seem wise, or line up with the Word? Are they reaping a harvest of righteousness and producing good fruit in their lives? If not, perhaps they are not praying or being led by the Spirit of God.

Having a relationship with God, praying, and knowing His voice are so imperative and a must whether single or married. God says when you pray in secret, you will be rewarded openly. There are two points to extract from this part of the scripture. First, God says *"when* you pray," which indicates that there is an expectation to do this. Prayer is a two-way conversation with God. We communicate with Him, and He communicates with us. Second, it's important to acknowledge where we pray and our motives for praying. Is it done privately between us and God, or is it a public spectacle? Now, the latter is not to be confused with corporate times of prayer. Many churches have set times to come together to seek God. Nothing wrong with that, but caution should also be exercised to avoid being like the hypocrites whose methods and motives were based upon being seen by others. Today, we have other public forums that can be used as a platform for us to garner attention. Yet, if we are not careful and our motives are not pure in communicating in public spaces, the reward we gain from that will go no further than likes, thumbs up, views, subscriptions, and other forms of personal or virtual validation.

When I consider the importance of prayer in relationships, I believe we should be in a place that we do not have to out-source our prayers. After you marry a person and a matter arises that requires prayer, can both you and your spouse reach God? When dating and an issue arises within your home or individual lives, do you or the person you are considering ALWAYS have to call someone else to pray? True, there are some instances where spiritual leaders or others who God puts on your heart should be contacted to touch and agree with you in prayer. But what happens on those occasions when no one else is available? I'll speak for myself and say that if I had to choose one thing that's important to me, it's knowing that a man can pray and be certain that his prayers are effectual, fervent, and availing **(Jm. 5:16b)**. Since prayer is a key factor in the life of the believer, my hope is that we grow in this area so that you don't have to phone a friend to hear from God.

There is so much that can be said about prayer. It will not all be addressed in this book, but I did want to take a moment to acknowledge how vital it is to both the life of the believer and in relationships. The takeaway from this chapter is this: Find out whether or not the man or woman you are with or are considering has a private prayer life. In your efforts to confirm this, don't violate them because what they're doing is sacred and is supposed to be done in secret. But again, find out if they're praying, if they hear from God, and most of all, if they obey God.

Chapter 6

CONFESSIONS

Proverbs 18:21 (NKJV)

> *Death and life are in the power of the tongue,*
> *and those who love it will eat its fruit.*

W e were created in God's image and likeness **(Gen. 1:26-27)**. Throughout the entire first chapter of Genesis, you see God saying, "Let there be …" then creating what He spoke and looking back at it to see that it was good and/or blessing His creation. Being made in the image and likeness of God means we too can be partakers of His creative power. With all of this in mind, my focus this chapter is on the tongue. What do you say? What do they say? What do you both believe and say about yourselves and others?

The old saying "Sticks and stones may break my bones, but words will never hurt me," is false! Words have power. They may not always have the immediate physical effect that sticks and stones have on the body, but the wrong words spoken to or about you can certainly do their fair share of damage. Think about a time you or someone you know were impacted by negative words. Can you recall a time when someone was lied about and experienced the repercussions of it? Have you or someone you know been told negative things about your physique and appearance, resulting in esteem issues or a warped view of yourself? It all goes back to words that were spoken. The same way positive words spoken can have a positive impact on people, places, and things, negative words spoken can negatively impact ourselves and others around us. Your words matter! Your words will shape your world.

I didn't realize how important it is to be aware of this quality in a relationship until I dated someone who did not have an awareness of the power of his words. Despite me imploring him to be mindful of what he said AND hearing this concept ministered over the pulpit together during the season we were in the relationship, he still did not seem to care. Although there were times he spoke positive things, which I applauded, there were too many negative things he spoke that I was not comfortable with. I recall his negative confessions concerning his body, age, and health. Although we were young and relatively healthy, he often made destructive comments in a joking nature about himself. I didn't share his sentiments and didn't want to be the companion of a person who I would have to take care of one day because he talked himself into physical degradation. I knew, as a possible future husband, this was one area in which I was not willing to compromise.

Luke 6:45 (NKJV) says, "A good man out of the good treasure of his heart brings forth good; and an evil man out of the evil treasure of his heart brings forth evil. For out of the abundance of the heart his mouth speaks." Ever wonder where negative talk comes from? The answer is clear. It comes from the heart! Positive speech comes from the heart as well. Whatever comes out of our mouths derives from within. Knowing this can give us and others insight into identifying what type of people we are. Don't try to separate people from the words they speak. If anything, their speech is an indicator of who they are at their core.

Although I'm constantly admonishing women to be attentive to the speech coming from men and future husbands, Proverbs brings light to the negative speech of a wife. **Proverbs 21:19 states, "Better to live in a desert than with a QUARRELSOME and NAGGING wife."** Now, this must be a bad situation for a man to want to leave his creature comforts for a dry, desolate, arid terrain to get away from his wife and her mouth! To be clear, I inserted this text to bring revelation to the impact of the words WE as women speak. This scripture may not fully depict the issue of negative confessions, but nevertheless, depending on what a wife is quarreling and nagging about, it's relevant. Remember, women, out of the abundance of the heart, the mouth speaks!

How can we separate ourselves from negative confessions we don't expect to come into fruition, while expecting the result of positive confessions we make? For example, I struggle when I hear many preachers say things like, "I'm in the wrong church!" or "I'm going to say this, but only five of ya'll are going to catch it." I've heard the second phrase stated over and over again in many churches I've visited, and only one time did I actually see this happen because the word spoken was specific, prophetic, and meant for the set number of people it was identified for.

However, when it comes to everything else being spoken to the congregation, do the speakers REALLY believe they're in the wrong church when people don't immediately react to what they've said? Is it true that ONLY five people in the entire fellowship are going to receive and comprehend the message being conveyed? These statements spoken over pulpits really bother me because I realize they are negative confessions over God's people. But before you get upset with me saying this, I know that they don't mean what they're saying. So, the question I want to pose is this—When they *do* mean what they are saying, especially when it's positive, how can we expect that to manifest for us and not the other? Do the words themselves have understanding and know when to work and when not to work? They don't send themselves; we send them. So, why have we trained ourselves to not believe what we say and to not be sensitive of the impact of the words we speak? This is not what we see God do. Imagine if God said things He didn't mean to us. What kind of life would we have? What kind of world would we live in? Again, our words shape our worlds.

You will have what you say! God designed us this way. God shows us time and time again in His Word that when we speak, things can and will happen if we don't doubt and we believe **(Mark 11:23)**. This is a part of the creative power bestowed upon us and the dominion we have over things in the earth. Please be mindful of the words you and others around you are speaking. Does the man or woman you are considering speak life and blessings into situations and create an atmosphere in which you can thrive? Do they speak death and curses that can ultimately lead to your demise? Do they speak a little life and a little death? Since we know that words have power, stop and consider the speech of others, and evaluate whether or not these are words you want to constantly linger in the atmosphere around you.

Additional scriptures for meditation:

Psalm 19:14 (NKJV)

Let the words of my mouth and the meditation of my heart be acceptable in Your sight, O Lord, my strength and my Redeemer.

Psalm 49:3 (NKJV)

My mouth shall speak wisdom, and the meditation of my heart shall give understanding.

James 3:7-12 (NLT)

[7] People can tame all kinds of animals, birds, reptiles, and fish, [8] but no one can tame the tongue. It is restless and evil, full of deadly poison. [9] Sometimes it praises our Lord and Father, and sometimes it curses those who have been made in the image of God. [10] AND SO BLESSING AND CURSING COME POURING OUT OF THE SAME MOUTH. SURELY, MY BROTHERS AND SISTERS, THIS IS NOT RIGHT! [11] Does a spring of water bubble out with both fresh water and bitter water? [12] Does a fig tree produce olives, or a grapevine produce figs? No, and you can't draw fresh water from a salty spring.

Chapter 7

CHOICES

Deuteronomy 30:19-20 (NKJV)

> ¹⁹ *"Today I have given you the choice between life and death, between blessings and curses. Now I call on heaven and earth to witness the choice you make. Oh, that you would choose life, SO THAT YOU AND YOUR DESCENDANTS MIGHT LIVE!* ²⁰ *You can make this choice by loving the LORD your God, obeying him, and committing yourself firmly to him. This is the key to your life. And if you love and obey the LORD, you will live long in the land the LORD swore to give your ancestors Abraham, Isaac, and Jacob."*

Although God was addressing the Children of Israel in this passage, we as believers today can glean that God has established the opportunity for us to make choices on a daily basis. He is not a puppet master, controlling our thoughts and deeds. Instead, He has given us a unique ability, and that's to choose the path we take in this life. The choices are VERY straightforward: life and death, blessings and curses. He loves us so passionately that He expressed His desire for us to choose life and receive all that comes with it. What kind of Creator would He be if He desired for us to choose death and all that is found along its path?

As individuals, it is so important that we practice making what I'll call "life choices" on a daily basis. Before we begin assessing our neighbor, can we make an honest assessment of the decisions and outcomes we have and are making in our own lives? There are both spiritual and natural things happening every day that have short-term and long-term effects, depending on our choices. Spiritually, we are presented with opportunities to obey or disobey the Word of God, study or not study the Bible, heed the voice of wisdom or go our own way. Naturally, we make decisions regarding whether or not to go to school or work, put healthy foods in our bodies or consume junk, spend time exercising or use our spare time lounging, etc. At the end of the day, the choices we make set us on course toward a particular destination. Once we're on that path, we cannot choose the consequences we encounter along the way.

So, how do the choices a person makes as a single believer translate into choices that will impact you in a relationship and marriage? Below is a list of a few things I've considered when it comes to this topic.

Do they:

- Worship God

- Study God's Word

- Communicate and demonstrate their personal relationship with Christ (i.e., through obeying His commands)

- Grow/respond to God's Word

- Pray

- Tithe

- Communicate with you and others well

- Respect or reject people in ANY position of authority

- Manage their money well

- Take care of themselves and their property

- Seek wisdom/counsel from God and others

- Make their own decisions (or are easily influenced by others)

- Deal with conflict by seeking resolution

- Use profanity/curse (life and death are in the power of the tongue)

- Enjoy their life

These are some of the areas that come to mind when I consider which choices to evaluate of another single believer. Your assessment should happen over time as you befriend and spend time with one another. This is critical because when you marry, the things you do and the choices you make impact others.

Generally, the choices you make will impact your immediate household first. And as the scriptures state, our choices will impact our generations **(Deut. 30:19, Ex. 20:5)**. Also remember, we are the body of Christ; therefore, some of the consequences of your choices impact the others you are connected to.

I'll give you another very practical example from the Bible. Genesis chapter 3 (NKJV) details the temptation and fall of man. After Eve was tempted by the serpent to eat the forbidden fruit, in her deception, she gave the same fruit to her husband, and in his disobedience to the Word of God, he ate it. As a result, God began to speak the following curses:

> [14] So the LORD God said to the serpent: "Because you have done this, you are cursed more than all cattle, and more than every beast of the field; on your belly you shall go, and you shall eat dust all the days of your life. [15] And I will put enmity between you and the woman, and between your seed and her Seed; He shall bruise your head, and you shall bruise His heel." [16] To the woman He said: "I will greatly multiply your sorrow and your conception; in pain you shall bring forth children; your desire shall be for your husband, and he shall rule over you." (For clarity, the Amplified version in verse 16 says, "**Yet your desire and** longing will be for your husband, **and he will rule [with authority] over you and** be responsible for you.")
>
> [17] Then to Adam He said, "Because you have heeded the voice of your wife, and have eaten

from the tree of which I commanded you, saying, 'You shall not eat of it': "Cursed is the ground for your sake; in toil you shall eat of it all the days of your life. ¹⁸ Both thorns and thistles it shall bring forth for you, and you shall eat the herb of the field. ¹⁹ In the sweat of your face you shall eat bread till you return to the ground, for out of it you were taken; for dust you are, and to dust you shall return."

Did you notice the three-fold impact of the choices made? The choices Eve made impacted herself, her husband, and their seed. **Also, the choice Adam made impacted himself and his seed.** Disobedience has a way of keeping you from the promises and presence of God. Let's not forget the serpent. The choice he made to deceive Eve rendered him cursed, on his belly, and with strife between his seed and Eve's.

If you look at the curse in reverse, there would be no enmity between the seeds, no pain in childbirth, no woman's desire for her husband, the husband wouldn't rule over his wife, no cursed ground, no toil ... Do you see where this is going? Ultimately, they were put outside of the Garden of Eden, and to this day, we are experiencing this curse. But thank God for the second Adam, Jesus Christ! It is through Him and the choices He made that we have redemption and salvation from this cursed state.

Do you see where our bad choices lead us? Clearly, "the wages of sin is death" **(Rom. 6:23)**. Though Adam and Eve didn't die a natural death immediately, the death they experienced was spiritual. They forfeited the wonderful benefits they had while in God's presence. The Bible says that the Enemy comes to kill, steal, and destroy **(John 10:10)**. Believe it or not, the Enemy desires to cause the same kind of death that happened to both Adam and Eve to happen in our lives. He does so by trying to deceive and influence us to make choices that are contrary to the Word and will of God for our lives.

Not all decisions have bad outcomes. However, all lead toward life or death, blessings or curses. Which have you chosen? Which will you choose? What choices have you observed others making? How will their choices impact you in a relationship?

After evaluating these things, you have another decision to make ... WHO will you choose?

Additional scriptures for meditation:

Deuteronomy 30:11-18

Proverbs 20:7 (NIV)

> **The righteous lead blameless lives; blessed are their children after them.**

CONCLUSION

Whether or not the topics in this book are areas you use to evaluate someone for a relationship, my goal was to present ideas so that you can reflect on what happens when you overlook who a person *is* for the sake of who he or she *could* be. We cannot hope and wish people into becoming better than who they present themselves to be. This takes introspection, reflection, and redirection of the individual to realize who he or she is and identify how he or she can improve and take action.

I hope you have found this book to be helpful, relevant, and thought-provoking. My prayer is that it will inspire discussions that will lead to meaningful changes in how dating and relationships are approached in our culture. My hope is that these changes will impact singles who desire to marry in a way that leads to better choices. My prayer is that when necessary, singles will be emboldened to leave unfruitful relationships and have the patience to wait upon the right person to embark upon the journey of a healthy marriage. Many blessings to you!

PRAYER OF SALVATION

Father,

Thank You for Your grace and mercy upon my life to live another day. Thank You for positioning me to receive Your Word and the opportunity accept Jesus as Lord and Savior. You sent Your Son into this world to die for our sins and bring eternal life to those who believe in Him. Today, I confess with my mouth that Jesus is Lord and believe in my heart that You raised Him from the dead. According to Your Word, I am saved! Thank You, Father, for Your gift of eternal life! Now, "Let the words of my mouth and the meditation of my heart be acceptable in Your sight, O LORD, my strength and my Redeemer" (Ps. 19:14).

Amen

CPSIA information can be obtained
at www.ICGtesting.com
Printed in the USA
BVHW041757160223
658686BV00012B/248